CONTEMPLATIVE COLORING

A Celtic Experience of the Gospel of Matthew

A Celtic Experience
of the Gospel of Matthew

Anamchara Books
Vestal, New York 13850
www.anamcharabooks.com

ISBN: 978-1-62524-473-4

Text edited by Kenneth McIntosh.
Illustration and design by Micaela Grace Sanna.

CONTEMPLATIVE COLORING

A Celtic Experience of the Gospel of Matthew

Anamchara Books

INTRODUCTION

Some 2,500 years ago, the group of people the ancient Greeks knew as the Celts were already expressing their beliefs about the world through a distinctive style of art. While their Greek contemporaries' art was increasingly realistic, the Celts decorated their dishes, their jewelry, their tools, and their weapons with sinuous abstract shapes and fantastic animals, designs that were rich with hidden meaning.

As the centuries passed, the Celts interacted with other cultures, and their art continued to evolve, while always keeping its distinctive interwoven patterns. In the islands that are now the United Kingdom, the Celts' creative style combined with Anglo-Saxon knotwork, creating an artistic fusion that was altogether new and different.

Then, as the Celts encountered the Gospels for the first time, they found a new source of creative inspiration. The designs they painted on their Gospel editions were not merely decoration. Archeology indicates that the early Christian Celts also had contact with Egypt's Christians, and art historians see in the Celts' illumined Gospels an artistic union that combined the ancient Celtic and Anglo Saxon designs with the characteristic style of Coptic icons, which were thought to be windows into the spiritual world.

Not everyone in the medieval world, however, agreed that art could function as a portal to God. In fact, many medieval theologians, including Augustine and Bonaventure, distrusted the visual arts. They believed that pictorial depictions of spiritual things were akin to the creation of idols.

Outside the Celtic world, the topic was fraught with controversy during the Middle Ages. The eighth-century French theologian, Theodolph, conceded that images can act as a "kind of ambassador," transmitting "memories to the soul." Two centuries earlier, Pseudo-Dionysius had written, "The Transcendent is clothed in the terms of being, with shape and form. . . . With these analogies we are raised upward." Those who defended the visual arts took this to mean that artistic images, like the Incarnation itself, were the means to "make the invisible visible." Bede, the seventh-century English historian, took a firm stand in this controversy, stating that images are a "living writing" that "open up, as it were, a living reading of the Lord's story."

Perhaps Bede was influenced by his close proximity to the Celts, who demonstrated so passionately the spiritual value of visual designs. At any rate, the early Christian Celts honored and celebrated Scripture as they interacted with it artistically. The production of their written Gospels was both artistic creation and an act of discovery. Creating these elaborate and time-consuming works of art was itself an act of spiritual devotion.

Today, many of us are rediscovering that creating with color and pattern can be both a spontaneous prayer and a spiritual ritual, one that leads us into remembrance of the Divine. Coloring creates a space in our busy lives for the gradual unfolding of our innermost being. It deepens our awareness of the present moment, and it opens us to insights and intuition.

Scientific research backs up these claims at the physiological level. When coloring, says psychologist Gloria Martínez Ayalan on her blog, we activate different areas of our two cerebral hemispheres. "The action involves both logic, by which we color forms, and creativity, when mixing and matching colors. This incorporates the areas of the cerebral cortex involved in vision and fine motor skills. The relaxation that it provides lowers the activity of the amygdala, a basic part of our brain involved in controlling emotion that is affected by stress."

Dr. Stan Rodski, a neuropsychologist who is also the author of his own line of adult coloring books, says that the act of coloring allows us to switch off our brains from other thoughts and be in the present moment. Rodski backs up this claim with medical technology. "The most amazing things occurred [when people were coloring]," he told the Australian Broadcasting Corporation. "We started seeing changes in heart rate, changes in brainwaves."

In fact, coloring produces many of the same brain changes that all meditation does. According to MRI studies done at Harvard University, the gray matter in our hippocampus increases—and the hippocampus is the part of the brain that helps us with self-awareness, compassion, and introspection. At the same time, changes to the amygdala help us to better manage anxiety and stress.

Coloring is good for our brains—and for our souls.

The images in this coloring book are taken from *The Winged Man: The Good News According to Matthew*, which is the first volume in Anamchara Books' Celtic Bible Commentary. Paired with each image is a short selection from the commentary, with a question to encourage a mental focal point as you color the image. Use this if it is helpful to you; disregard it if it isn't. Space has been provided for you to jot down any thoughts that the rise to the surface as you color—but keep in mind that the point of this book is not to write but to color (not to shape words but to engage in a wordless act of creation). It is an opportunity to participate in the Celtic view of reality.

We tend to categorize and recognize distinctions, but the Celts saw things differently. Their perception of the world did not, however, merge everything into a single uniform whole. Instead, in the same way that their designs twisted and twirled and twined, they also interlaced realities, weaving them together so that weft and warp meshed into something far richer and more colorful than the individual strands alone. As they illustrated the Gospels, the Celtic mind found ways to plait together past and present, earth and heaven, along with the world of their ancestors and the new culture they were encountering.

As we color these images, we begin to experience a similar unifying perception of a living spiritual reality. Scripture weaves its way into our consciousness, and we experience biblical images at a more deeply personal level. Our hearts are interlaced with the stories of Christ and his disciples.

Through the creation of images, wrote Pseudo-Dionysius, we can be "attuned to the divine harmony" and brought "into accord not only with divine realities but with ourselves and with others." As our hand moves across the paper, we engage in meditation in motion—and as our physical eyes feast on color and shape, our inner vision is cleared and sharpened. We glimpse the presence of God.

The ancient symbol for the Gospel of Matthew—a winged man—
has a deep spiritual significance that our modern minds may over-
look. While we equate winged human forms with angels, ancient
civilizations, including the Celts', perceived wings as a symbol for
an embodied connection with a wider and deeper reality.

For the Celts, the winged man was a seer, someone with the ability
to fly into the Otherworld and return, bringing with him new vision
to share with the more earthbound members of his society. He was
both a seeker of wisdom and the proclaimer of truth, a custodian
and guardian of divine insight.

*Where do you perceive the
presence of "wings" in your life?*

The Celts truly honored, celebrated, and interacted with the Word, in a way few of us have ever dreamed, bringing to the Gospel text their artistic skill, emotional intensity, and an expansive and inclusive imagination, all combined with a sense of creative freedom. They were following no rules, no established tradition. All was fresh and new.

How might your ideas about the Bible change if you could see it as something fresh and new, as the Celts' did?

The "Monogram Page" in the Book of Kells, consists entirely of the Chi Rho that was the abbreviation for Christ. Intertwined with the calligraphy of the letters themselves are circles within circles, triskelions, human faces, angels, an otter eating a fish, and a mother cat with her kittens. These images, which for the Celts were part of the entire experience of contemplating this first chapter of Matthew, indicate the all-encompassing enormity of the Incarnation.

Does your vision of the Incarnation need to be expanded?

Is a belief in a miraculous virgin birth necessary for us to believe in the Incarnation? That question has plagued Christians for centuries. In some instances, the virgin birth has been pulled out from the entire story as the fulcrum on which the whole Gospel rests. Modern Christianity has struggled with the seeming contradictions between science and a literal understanding of various biblical accounts (and not only in regards to the virgin birth). Medieval Celtic Christians also experienced this struggle, but with sometimes different conclusions. It was quite possible, some concluded, to believe passionately and wholeheartedly in the Incarnation, while still applying a scientific mind to the details of the story recounted in Matthew 1.

What does the birth of Jesus mean to you?

Just as God used Pagan sorcerers to honor and serve the baby Jesus, in the same way God used the pre-Christian druids to anticipate the coming of the Gospel. As Thomas O'Loughlin explains in his book *Celtic Theology*, "It is not a case of Christianity walking into a void—into a place where God is not, where religion is not, culture is not—nor into a place where the Spirit has not been at work." God was already there.

Are there place in our world today where
you have failed to see the presence of God?

John the Baptist is a wild and wooly figure, the incendiary preacher who is clad in skins and lives off the land. In today's world, he would be the long-haired, bearded hippie who wanders out of the wilds into a city square. Though John is a fascinating character, he remains a minor one when compared to the center of Matthew's story: Jesus. In church art, John the Baptist is always portrayed pointing—to Christ, whom he baptizes. In Matthew, John the Baptist declares, "He who comes after me is mightier than I" (3:11). ✦

If you were to meet John the Baptist, what would he say to you?

When a young woman fell in love with Saint Kevin of Glendalough, the story goes, she "endeavoured to engage the love of this holy youth, by her looks, her words, and sometimes, by her messages"—but Kevin perceived her as a temptation to stray from his path as a celibate monk. Although he steadfastly rejected the young woman, she continued to pursue him. Kevin retained his celibacy, but in the process, he doesn't seem so pious. The story goes on to say that one day, when the woman followed him into the woods, Kevin took a bundle of nettles and began to strike her. Clearly, Kevin blamed the woman for his temptation. Instead of acknowledging his physical urge to use this woman sexually, he projected his own sinfulness onto her.

Before we dismiss this as merely a tale indicative of medieval misogyny, we might want to examine our own hearts. When we are angry, do we acknowledge our interior selfishness—or do we blame the person who "made" us angry?

What have you projected onto others that is coming from your own heart?

"Change your lives! For the Reign of Heaven is at hand." (Matthew 4:7)

How are you being called to change?

The Celtic hermit "deliberately chosen to live at the limits of existence, a human person containing both heaven and earth." 

How can your life be stretched to include both heaven and earth?

When he got into a boat, his disciples followed him. Then a violent storm came up on the sea, so much that the boat was covered with the waves, but he was asleep. His disciples came to him, and woke him up, saying, "Save us, Great One! We are dying!"

He said to them, "Why are you fearful, O you of little faith?" Then he got up, rebuked the wind and the sea, and there was a great calm. (Matthew 8:23–26)

What is making you fearful?

The life of Saint Patrick illustrates God's Spirit continuing to speak through human lives. After escaping slavery in Ireland, Patrick was called back there to bring the people the Good News of Jesus, because, he wrote, he heard the Spirit praying "in my inner man."

What is the Spirit praying in your inner being?

Patrick's *Confessions* indicate the connection between listening to God's voice and being able to speak Divine truth ourselves. He recorded a time in his life when he was full of despair—and then was inspired and strengthened by the Spirit's presence in the natural world: "The splendor of the sun fell on me; and immediately, all that weight was lifted from me. I believe that I was helped by Christ the Lord, and that his Spirit cried out for me. I trust that it will be like this whenever I am under stress." Patrick went on to quote Matthew 10:20: "It is not you speaking, but the Spirit of your Abba who speaks in you."

Where do you feel the presence of the Spirit in your life?

After years of slavery, Patrick found courage and identity in his Spirit-given powers of speech. "I was a silent stone," he wrote, "unable to speak, lying squashed in the mud, when the Mighty and Merciful God came, dug me out, and set me on top of the wall. Therefore, I praise him." As we listen to God's voice, speaking to us in Nature, in Scripture, through others, and through our own hearts and minds, we too can find a new, more courageous, and more authentic form of speech. "What I tell you in the darkness," Jesus says in Matthew 10:27, "speak in the light; and what you hear whispered in the ear, proclaim on the housetops."

What might you speak in the light?
What is your authentic voice?

The eight-century historian Bede tells in *The Ecclesiastical History of the English People* of the ancient Celtic tradition of the "Passing of the Harp," where communities would gather in the mead hall, or other communal space, and tell stories through the evenings around a fire, with food and drink flowing. The Celts have always understood the powerful properties of stories to speak hidden truths. For them, stories were sacred, capable of revealing God to us in new and surprising ways, and Jesus used parables in the same way. In his parables, we hear "things hidden from the foundation of the world," so that we might perceive with our eyes, hear with our ears, understand with our hearts, and turn again to God to be healed.

What story will you tell the world?

Those who seek their life will lose it; and any who lose their life for my sake will find it. (Matthew 10:39)

Are you seeking your life?
Are you willing to lose your life?

Jesus went out of the house, and sat by the seaside. Great crowds gathered around him, so he boarded a boat, where he sat while the crowd stood on the beach. He spoke to them many things in parables. (Matthew 13:1–3)

What might Jesus be saying to you in your life today? Are you hearing any "parables"?

Peter stepped down from the boat, and walked on the waters to come to Jesus. But when he saw that the wind was strong, he was afraid and beginning to sink, he cried out, saying, "Great One, save me!"

Immediately, Jesus stretched out his hand, took hold of him, and said to him, "You of little faith, why did you doubt?" (Matthew 14:29–31)

What might you do if you could "walk on water"?

As modern readers, when we read these stories of miraculous feeding, we are likely to see a reassuring symbolism that speaks to us of God's ability to meet our needs, to multiply our meager resources so that we have enough. The Christian Celts also read this meaning into the story, but unlike us, they focused on the disciples' role as well. For them, the story had a twofold meaning, speaking of Otherworldly providence while equally emphasizing that humans are to do their share in this Divine work. "The good of the loaves and fishes," says one blessing, "as God divided them. . . . Good fortune from the King who made the division, on our share and on our co-division."

How can you do your share of God's work in the world around you?

Early Celtic Christians interpreted Jesus' call to "take up the cross" (Matthew 16:24) in practical ways that we may find overly literal. Irish monks would often pray with their arms straight out from their sides in the shape of a cross, sometimes praying for hours in this uncomfortable pose atop a windswept hill or in the waters of a lake or stream. This was known as the Cross-Vigil, a practice that the monks believed allowed them to obey Jesus' challenge. For us, this seems like an extreme interpretation, but the Celtic saints were enacting the Gospel with their physical bodies.

One day, the story goes, as Saint Kevin was praying the Cross-Vigil in his cell, with his arms outstretched and a hand resting on the windowsill, a blackbird perched on his palm and then began constructing her nest there. Kevin held perfectly still while she finished her nest and settled down to lay her eggs. Kevin was so filled with tenderness for the bird, we are told, that he remained immobile, his hand outstretched, until the eggs hatched and the nestlings ventured forth.

Can you see the living Cross in the world of Nature?

The eye of the great God
The eye of the God of glory
The eye of the King of hosts
The eye of the King of the living
Pouring upon us
At each time and season
Pouring upon us
Gently and generously
Glory to thee
Thou Glorious Sun
Glory to thee, thou Sun
Face of the God of Life.
(Carmina Gadelic)

What does the sun say to your heart?

What is clear *is* that Jesus was far more condemning of people who abused and exploited society's helpless and vulnerable individuals, whether they were children (Matthew 19:14) or the poor (Matthew 19:21), than he was of people who violated sexual mores.

Do you harbor any prejudice in your heart?

"If you want to be perfect, go, sell what you have, and give to the poor, and you will have treasure in heaven. Then come, follow me."
(Matthew 19:21)

*What might Jesus ask you to surrender
so that you can be free to follow him?*

Almighty God,
Father, Son, and Holy Spirit,
to me the least of saints,
to me allow that I may keep even the smallest door,
the farthest, darkest, coldest door,
the door that is least used, the stiffest door,
if only it be in Your house, O God,
that I can see Your glory afar,
and hear Your voice,
and know that I am with You,
O God.
(St. Columba)

What door leads you into God's presence?

"Tell the daughter of Zion,
behold, your Sovereign comes to you,
humble, and riding on a donkey,
on a colt, the foal of a donkey."
(Matthew 21:5)

What would you do were you to see
Jesus riding toward you on a donkey?

Saint Brigid, perhaps the most beloved of all Celtic saints, had much in common with Jesus. With total disregard for property law, she gave away her father's belongings to the poor; she tricked the King of Leinster into giving her a large portion of land for her monastery; and she regularly gave to the poor from the farms and kitchens where she worked. Despite her constant mischief for good, Brigid always evades the grasp of the stingy authority figures. Like Jesus, she taps into a supernatural stream of power, but also like him, she demonstrates plenty of human intelligence, insight, and craftiness.

How do the supernatural and the practical interact in your life?

Brigid is like Jesus in another way. In verse 32, Jesus indicates that God is a God of the present tense—and God's people also exist in that same Holy Now. The Reign of Heaven that Jesus describes is not something that lies in the future; it cannot be considered the *after*-life, for it is the *now*-life. In the old stories, Brigid has a similar disregard for the boundaries of time. She slips into the past (and around the globe) to act as Mary's midwife and Jesus' babysitter; she also travels more than three centuries forward in time to chat with a dying man, comforting him during his last hours.

Do you sense the Reign of Heaven in your now-life?

Heaven is coming to us now, in this moment, Jesus says (Matthew 24:42, 44). The Heaven of which he's speaking has nothing to do with streets of gold and pie in the sky. Instead, it's a place of integrity and justice, a living and practical reality that challenges us to be true to God, to others, to the Earth, and to our own souls.

Can you see Heaven coming to you in this moment?

Jesus calls us to live in the here-and-now, rather than postponing our response to his challenge for some later, more convenient day. He asks us to be in a state of constant readiness (Matthew 24:46), what a Buddhist might describe as mindfulness. At any moment, Heaven's demands can erupt into our lives.

Does Heaven have room to blossom in your life?

Every time we give to those in need, we are giving to Jesus. Giving to others was an ancient custom of the Celts, as well as among many peoples. It is a sure demonstration of love, not only for others but also for God. Jesus makes clear that the two cannot be separated. We cannot say we love God if we are not actively engaged in showing love—in concrete, practical ways—to those around us.

*How can you love those around you—
in practical, tangible ways?*

Saint Brigid never tried to convert anyone using the "Four Spiritual Laws"; she never talked about sin and hell, nor tried to persuade others to "give their hearts to Jesus." Instead, she attended to their physical needs, spreading God's love in practical ways. Her example challenges us: What are we to be doing with our body on this earth? How do we treat others and their bodies? However we answer these questions will say much about our relationship with Jesus (Matthew 25:45).

Do you treat your body and others' bodies as though they were the body of Jesus?

Tales also abound of the quiet acceptance and faith of Celtic saints in the presence of approaching death, which they often saw in advance. Their lives focused on finding their "place of resurrection," in which they could best await entry to heaven and pray for those making the same journey.

Have you found your place of resurrection?

In the Garden of Gethsemane, Jesus prays that he might be spared having to drink from the "cup" that awaits him (Matthew 25:39, 42). Today, we have an ongoing fascination with the mythological cup Jesus drank from, known in Arthurian legend as the Grail, which has been interpreted as everything from a symbol for the Divine Feminine, to a Celtic vessel of plenty, to an archetype for individual fulfillment. Jesus' prayer in the Garden points us in a different direction. He has already shared the actual "cup" with his disciples at the Last Supper (Matthew 25:27), and the metaphorical cup he refers to now is the death that lies ahead of him. Ultimately, he accepts from his Abba the cup that is, as Bonhoeffer said as he went to his execution, "the end," which is also "the beginning of life."

Do you see your death as the beginning of a new life?

The theory of the cross most modern Christian denominations hold is that of "substitution." This theory goes like this: all humans are sinners who deserve God's wrath, but Jesus' death satisfied the cost of human sin. The Celts understood the crucifixion quite differently; their understanding was based on the perspective of the "Christus Victor" model of atonement. The Christus Victor premise was that Jesus' death was not a legal settlement with God (where God had to punish someone for human sin, so Jesus substituted himself for humanity) but instead a victorious battle against the forces of darkness. On the cross, Christ stepped into the human arena where we all confront death and the other works of Satan. Like the bravest of knights, he fought with these terrifying enemies and was triumphant; he forced them to release humanity from their grip.

What does the cross of Jesus mean to you?

For the ancient Celts, the cross was a symbol of Christ's heroic and eternal victory over hell and death. They believed if they descended to the very depths of hell, they would find the cross waiting for them, offering them hope and salvation even there.

Can you find the cross in the "hells" you have experienced?

The Celtic saints identified with Jesus death on the cross as a way for them to offer up their own lives in the battle against evil. They joyfully chose to join their Hero as he hung from the cross. And they kept tangible signs of the cross always nearby, and they claimed the cross as part of their daily lives, an aspect of their most intimate identities.

Is the meaning of the cross part of your daily life?

Christ's cross over this face I wear, and over my ear.
Christ's cross over my eye.
Christ's cross over my nose.
Christ's cross to accompany me before.
Christ's cross to accompany me behind me.
Christ's cross to meet every difficulty both on hollow and hill
Christ's cross over me as I sit.
Christ's cross over me as I lie.
Christ's cross be all my strength until we reach the King of Heaven.
From the top of my head to the end of my toenail,
O Christ, against every danger I trust in the protection of the cross.
Till the day of my death, when my flesh goes into the clay,
And I shall once more take
Christ's cross over this face.

*What might it mean to wear
Christ's cross across your face?*

The centurion said, "Truly this was the Son of God."
(Matthew 27:54)

Do you believe that Jesus was God's son?

Saint Patrick's beliefs made him more aware of the preciousness of this world. They gave him a sense of urgency about building Heaven's realm on earth. ⊕

Are you building Heaven's realm on earth?

For the Celtic saints, the Reign of Heaven had already begun, now, in the present moment, in the ordinary world. In a story from Ireland's oral tradition, Patrick's farewell to a friend illustrates that perspective. "From myself to yourself," Patrick says, "in the house or out of the house, in whatever place God will lay His hand on you, I give you Heaven."

Where do you find Heaven in your ordinary life?

Jesus' presence means the Reign of Heaven is here and now. We are each a valuable part of the great, ongoing tale that extends from the Jesus who walked the earth more than two thousand years ago, to Patrick's medieval mission, to the twenty-first-century and beyond. We are actors, each with a vital and urgent role to play, in Heaven's continuing story.

What role do you play in Heaven's story?

"I am with you always, even to the end of the age." (Matthew 28:20)

Do you sense Jesus' presence with you?

CELTIC BIBLE COMMENTARY

⚇ Sometimes, illumination from the ancient past can reveal the road ahead. ⚇

Each volume of the Celtic Bible Commentary contains a new translation of that book of the Bible, with commentaries, written by Celtic and Bible scholars, for all chapters. These commentaries include insights from the ancient Celts—and apply them to our own lives in the twenty-first century, challenging us to weave the Bible's stories into our own. Each commentary encourages us to read scripture "the Celtic way," encountering it as fresh, living, and radical.

For the Celts, the Bible was something amazing and wondrous. It was to be read attentively, with the commitment and fascination the lover feels for the beloved. Their approach to reading scripture need not be lost to us. We too can learn to open our hearts and minds to the gift of the Divine Word, allowing the Breath of God to inspire us and transform us in unpredictable ways—and then sweep through us like a flame that kindles new life and healing in the world around us.

THE WINGED MAN:
The Good News According to Matthew
CELTIC BIBLE COMMENTARY: VOLUME TWO

Paperback Price: $24.99
E-book Price: $9.99
ISBN: 978-1-62524-472-7

Matthew's version of the Good News is traditionally symbolized by a winged man, because the author saw Jesus as fulfilling two roles. On the one hand, he is the Divine One who proclaims that the Realm of Heaven is present in the here and now—and on the other hand, he is the Human One, who shares our physical reality. In Matthew's account, Jesus, like a winged man, represents the union of human and Divine qualities. This first volume of the Celtic Bible Commentary brings these ideas to life. When the Celtic followers of Jesus read Matthew's Gospel, they did not see it as dead text codified in ancient times but rather as a chance to interlace their own hearts with the living story of Jesus. For them, this portion of scripture was truly a winged man who brought good news from heaven to earth. The Realm of Heaven is all around us—and Matthew's account calls us to experience it for ourselves. ⊕

THE WINGED LION:
The Good News According to Mark
CELTIC BIBLE COMMENTARY: VOLUME TWO

Paperback Price: $24.99
E-book Price: $9.99
ISBN: 978-1-62524-468-0

In the fifth century, Saint Jerome assigned to each of the four Gospel authors a winged creature that is still associated with that particular account of the life of Jesus. Mark's symbol is a winged lion, an image of courage and triumph, representing Christ's authority over life and death. With the Celtic saints, we find in this Gospel a vision of Jesus that is always larger than anything we have experienced in ordinary life—a vision that challenges us to live life in a new and deeper way.

THE WINGED CALF:
The Good News According to Luke
CELTIC BIBLE COMMENTARY: VOLUME THREE

Paperback Price: $24.99
E-book Price: $9.99
ISBN: 978-1-62524-469-7

The Gospel author we know as Luke is traditionally represented by a winged calf, a figure of otherworldly sacrifice, service, and strength. This account of Jesus' life begins with the sacrificial duties of Zacharias in the temple, and it focuses on Christ's self-giving on the Cross. The Gospel of the Calf struck a chord that resonated in the heart of Celtic faith. For the Celts, this was a metaphor that embraced the deepest meaning of Christian life—giving ourselves away on behalf of others. As one ancient Celtic author put it, "A person who has compassion for the needs of neighbors truly carries the cross." Luke's Gospel points us toward the Way of Jesus, the way of the calf.

THE FAR-SEEING EAGLE:
The Good News According to John
CELTIC BIBLE COMMENTARY: VOLUME FOUR

Paperback Price: $24.99
E-book Price: $9.99
ISBN: 978-1-62524-470-3

John's symbolic animal is an eagle, a far-seeing creature of the sky that was believed to be able to look straight into the sun. The author of this Gospel differed from the others in that he describes Jesus as the eternal Word, focusing throughout his account on Jesus' Divine nature. The same man who walked the streets of Nazareth, writes John, is also the universe-filling Wisdom of God who existed from the beginning of Creation. For the Celts, who loved seeing more-than-literal meaning throughout the Bible, this Gospel is a treasure trove of symbolism. As we read it, we too are challenged to live differently but also to see differently, to perceive the deep spiritual Mystery that is hidden everywhere we look.

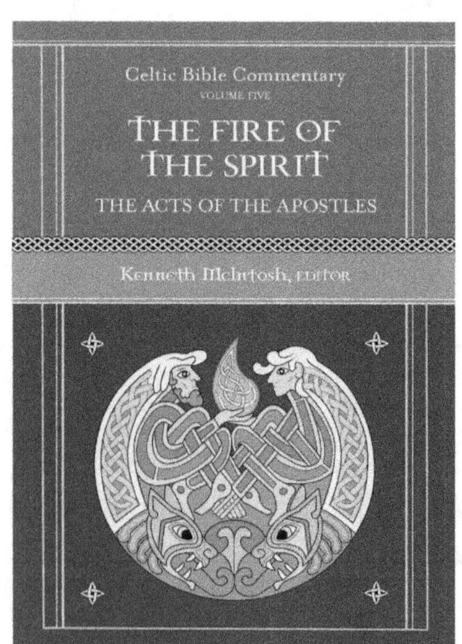

THE FIRE OF THE SPIRIT:
The Acts of the Apostles
CELTIC BIBLE COMMENTARY: VOLUME FIVE

Paperback Price: $24.99
E-book Price: $9.99
ISBN: 978-1-62524-471-0

Although this book is traditionally titled "The Acts of the Apostles," a better title might be "The Acts of the Holy Spirit." In Acts, God's Breath (or Spirit) does not descend as the traditional dove but instead falls as fire. The Spirit's flaming presence is the motif for Pentecost, and afterward Spirit spreads like wildfire from Jerusalem outward, transforming lives as it advances. Acts is an account of how people came to believe in the Way of Jesus, but it is even more the story of how Spirit brought people to venture beyond their traditional religious boundaries. Throughout Acts, the inclusive Breath of God works continually to break down barriers erected by prejudice, ego, or insecurity. The ancient Christian Celts opened their hearts to this message, and they challenge us to join the Spirit in extending God's welcome to everyone, without exception.